MW00397111

THE EMERGENCY RESPONSE

COMMUNICATIONS HANDBOOK

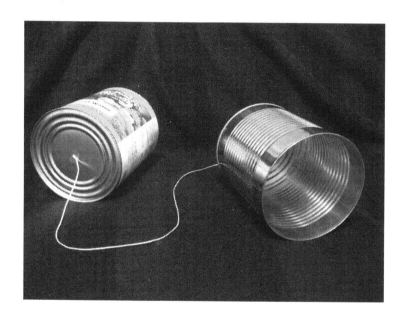

Dennis A. Bartholomew, AF6TR

Published by Dennis A. Bartholomew
Sacramento, California

Copyright © 2013 by Dennis Bartholomew

All rights reserved. No part of this book may be reproduced in any format or in any medium without the written permission of the publisher. This work is not an official publication of the Church of Jesus Christ of Latter Day Saints. The views expressed within this work are the sole responsibility of the author and do not necessarily reflect the position of The Church of Jesus Christ of Latter Day Saints or any other entity.

Printed in the United States of America
First Printing: January 2013
V2

18 17 16 15 14   12 11 10 9 8 7 6 5 4 3 2 1

ISBN-13:
978-1477689202

ISBN-10:
1477689206

TABLE OF CONTENTS

INTRODUCTION

This handbook is designed for those who are interested in emergency communications. It is directed primarily toward members of the Church of Jesus Christ of Latter-day Saints, but many portions apply to anyone interested in emergency communications in general. Those who would benefit most from this book are LDS Church Priesthood leaders such as stake presidencies, bishoprics and high counselors who are responsible for emergency preparedness and emergency communications, as well as those called or assigned specifically to positions which pertain to emergency preparedness and emergency communications.

For your benefit, its contents are assembled to provide you with all the information which will help you understand how emergency communications operate within the Church. After reading this book, you will have a more complete understanding of how to communicate when other conventional forms of communications are unavailable.

DISCLAIMER

While some quotes will be provided from LDS scriptures and official Church sources, this work is not a publication of the Church of Jesus Christ of Latter-day Saints. The author is solely responsible for its content.

THE IMPORTANCE OF COMMUNICATIONS IN EMERGENCIES

History has proven many times that during disasters, normal forms of communication such as telephone, cell service and the internet, are not available. If the future is anything like the past, there will be times when conventional methods of communication are compromised again. We often take normal means of communication for granted. Being able to communicate is a daily human need. When there is an emergency, communication is even more important. In fact, it is vital.

We will explore the various types of emergency communications, how to use them, which methods work best and under what circumstances, what is expected of communicators, and many other subjects that relate to the general subject of emergency communications and preparedness within the LDS Church.

In the Church, many people struggle with an emergency communications calling or assignment. Some don't receive the needed support from their Priesthood leaders. Others find it difficult to learn the intricacies of amateur radio (also called 'ham' radio). Still others see no need for emergency communication at all. These and other challenges will be addressed in this book, and will provide a comprehensive and helpful reference to those challenges.

WHAT DOES THE CHURCH SAY ABOUT EMERGENCY COMMUNICATIONS?

Many Church leaders have spoken about this subject. Here is one example –

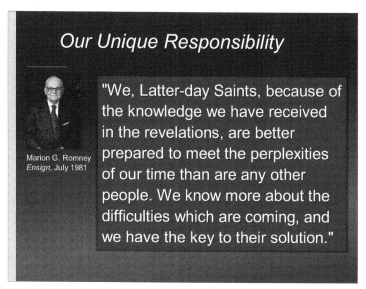

Our Unique Responsibility

Marion G. Romney
Ensign, July 1981

"We, Latter-day Saints, because of the knowledge we have received in the revelations, are better prepared to meet the perplexities of our time than are any other people. We know more about the difficulties which are coming, and we have the key to their solution."

The Church of Jesus Christ of Latter-day Saints has provided direction regarding the calling or assigning of emergency communications persons. For official information, go to the Church's web site. The direct link is

http://www.lds.org/topics/emergency-preparedness/guidelines-for-emergency-communication?lang=eng

You can navigate to it by going to lds.org and click on Resources, then Home and Family. Click on Preparing for Emergencies. Then click on Emergency Communications. You can click on Guidelines for Emergency Communication or Frequently Asked Questions on Emergency Communication. As with most web sites, changes take place frequently. If you are unable to locate the information by using the directions above, just use the Search feature on lds.org by entering the term Emergency Communication. Following are the guidelines provided:

During an emergency, normal means of communication may become inoperable. Priesthood leaders should consider:

- How to contact missionaries and members following a disaster.

- How to communicate the status of missionaries, members, buildings, and other necessary information to area leaders.

- Available communication personnel and equipment

Communication Specialists

Priesthood leaders may call communication specialists as needed. Individuals interested in communications often own radio equipment and possess valuable experience.

Additional Resources

SATELLITE TELEPHONES – Some storehouses in the United States and Canada have satellite telephones. In other Church areas, satellite telephones are available in administration offices for emergency use.

AMATEUR RADIO – Some storehouses in the United States and Canada have amateur radio equipment and conduct regular network exercises. For information, contact your Priesthood leader or regional welfare specialist.

The guidelines above will be referenced in the next chapter.

LET'S HAVE A PLAN

The first action in preparing for any emergency is to have a plan. The bishop and stake president may wish to call or assign an individual to formulate an emergency plan. A guideline is on the Church's web site.

The exact link is:

https://www.lds.org/bc/content/shared/content/english/pdf/welfar e/stake-ward-emergency-planning-guide-eng.pdf

This document can be accessed by going to **www.lds.org** and clicking on Resources. Then click on Home and Family under the Family Category. Click on Preparing for Emergencies, then on the right, click on Stake and Ward Emergency Planning Guide. If the guide is not available through the above link, perform a search at lds.org using the phrase, Stake and Ward Emergency Planning Guide. Its contents are as follows. Please note that comments by the author follow each of the five following steps. They are in italics.

Stake and Ward Emergency Planning Guide

Stake and ward councils can use this planning guide to create or update emergency response plans (see Handbook 1: Stake Presidents and Bishops [2010] 5.1.3 and 5.2.11). Stake and ward plans should be coordinated with plans in the community. Leaders may consider calling welfare specialists to assist with emergency response efforts. The most effective plans are brief and not overly complex. It is recommended that councils review and update plans regularly.

Step 1: Identify Likely Disasters

List the disasters (natural or man-made) that are most likely to occur in your area. For each type of disaster, identify specific response actions that would be needed. (For example: In a disaster that can damage homes—such as an earthquake, fire, flood, or hurricane—a key action would be to find temporary shelter for displaced families.)

The possible disasters that come to mind are – fire, flood, earthquake, chemical spill, extended power loss, civil disturbance, pandemic/epidemic, dirty bomb, war or nuclear attack, resulting in radiation or an EMP event (the last of which is discussed in the chapters on page 55, 73 and 79).

Step 2: Gather Critical Information

Compile and maintain the following information:

- Contact data for all members and missionaries living within stake or ward boundaries.

- A map of the area, including the locations of member and missionary residences.

- A list of members with special needs, such as the disabled and the elderly.

A list of members with equipment or skills (such as medical or emergency response training) that would be critical in a disaster.

- Contact information for public safety agencies (e.g., police, fire, medical).

- Contact information for community organizations (e.g., the Red Cross or Red Crescent) that provide emergency services, such as food, shelter, and medical care.

- Contact information for area welfare leaders and, where available, local Church welfare operations.

All lists and maps should be on paper in the event that computers or power are not available. If power is available, copies can be made of these lists, if needed. In other words, don't rely on electronic forms of ward lists, maps, etc. A hard copy of the ward roster, and other lists as desired, should be a part of the ward or stake emergency plan. All lists and maps should be updated at least twice per year. Ward and stake maps and directories are available at lds.org by signing in and clicking on All Tools, then Maps. Incidentally, the Red Cross is called the Red Crescent in some parts of the world.

Step 3: Outline Assignments and Procedures

Plan how the council will organize and carry out each of the tasks listed below, identifying who will be responsible for each and what procedures they will follow. Designate a primary and an alternate central location where council members will gather after an emergency to direct relief efforts.

Prior to a disaster –

- Develop working relationships with civil authorities and other community relief organizations.

Immediately after a disaster –

- Determine and report the condition of members and missionaries.

- Reports on member needs generally come from home teachers to quorum leaders, who then report them to the bishop. Bishops, in turn, report them to the stake president.

- Help to locate and reunite family members who have become separated.

- Obtain medical care for those who have been injured or who have other health challenges.

- Coordinate response efforts with civil authorities and community relief organizations.

- Assess needs and arrange for the supply of basic provisions and services—such as food, temporary shelter, sanitation, and clothing—for members and others.

- Area welfare leaders and, where available, Church welfare operations can be called upon to assist with provisions and services.

- Determine and report the condition of Church buildings and property.

In the period following a disaster –

- Provide assistance to members who have suffered damage to homes or belongings, emotional trauma, or loss of livelihood.

11

- Work with civil authorities and relief organizations to identify and respond to opportunities for the Church to assist with community needs.

On bullet point 1, this cannot be over emphasized. Relationships with outside agencies are always encouraged and should be cultivated long before the need arises. On bullet point 2, missionaries are a priority. The reason is that the parents of missionaries may hear of a disaster in your area and not have any method of contacting them. In addition, when normal means of communication are not available, the message will take much longer to get to Church Headquarters and ultimately, their families. If their status is determined quickly, the information can be forwarded sooner.

Step 4: Identify Emergency Communication Methods

Identify and plan for alternative communication methods that can be used in case phone lines, cellular phone service, or vehicle transportation routes are disrupted during a disaster. Such methods may include:

- Internet communications (including e-mail, social media, and Internet telephony).

- Text messaging via cellular phone (which may be available even if voice service is not).

- Amateur radio.

- Personal contact via foot, bicycle, etc. (Full-time missionaries can also help.)

As needed, Priesthood leaders may call members of their units to be communication specialists. Qualified specialists often own communications equipment and possess valuable experience.

This is the central theme of communications specialists. As stated in the Church's guide, use any and all forms of communications that are practical. It has been said that "it's better to have a deacon on a dirt bike than a bishop in a Buick." This allows the bishop to be in the proper location – his emergency headquarters, wherever that may be. There are other forms of practical communication. Each ward or stake is different in size and topography. Various other methods are discussed on page 21.

Step 5: Encourage Member Preparation

Regularly encourage members to engage in preparedness efforts and to follow the counsel outlined in the pamphlets All Is Safely Gathered In:

Family Home Storage (04008) and All Is Safely Gathered In: Family Finances (04007).

Channels for doing this might include:

• Quorum and Relief Society meetings.
• Sacrament meeting or stake conference talks.
• Home and visiting teaching messages.

Most members are aware of the Church's desire to have all members prepared. It is sometimes a matter of slow progress. For example, a home teacher can suggest that his families gradually build up their 72 hour kit. Each month, they can add one or two items that are suggested by the home teacher.

Another meeting that can be used for emergency preparation and communication training and awareness is the fifth Sunday joint meeting. You can volunteer to give a presentation at this class time when you are comfortable with the subject matter. Another meeting, one on the stake level, is the monthly bishop's meeting with the stake president. This can be a productive meeting because the subject matter is endorsed by the stake president. This gives you the opportunity to provide the bishops in the stake with the same message. The author is aware of bishops and stake presidents who have obtained their own ham radio licenses. This has a big advantage in that these Priesthood leaders are stalwart supporters of emergency communications.

UTILIZING MLS AS PART OF THE PLAN

MLS, or Member Leader System is the computer program that is used in each branch, ward and stake to maintain membership records. It has some features that can be used for emergency planning. A section called Household Geocode provides the preparedness specialist a tool which allows the ward or branch to be divided into smaller sections, sometimes called neighborhoods. These sections are organized by concentration of members and natural barriers, such as rivers, canals, major streets, etc. Usually, no more than ten neighborhoods are necessary for organizing a ward or branch. After determining the borders for each section, unique names for the sections can be created and entered into the Geocode system. The names are attached to each household. Once this has been accomplished, it is possible to print each section separately, providing lists of member households by section or neighborhood. This allows for easy planning when it is necessary to go to each member's home. A leader may be assigned to each section. This person is sometimes called a Section Leader or Block Captain.

THE SPECIFIC CALLING / ASSIGNMENT OF COMMUNICATIONS SPECIALISTS

As stated in the Church's web site under Guidelines for Emergency Communication, "Priesthood leaders may call communication specialists as needed. Individuals interested in communications often own radio equipment and possess valuable experience."

Under the direction of your Priesthood leader, you, as the communications specialist should work closely with the emergency preparedness specialist. These two assignments are hand-in-glove assignments. Those called as preparedness and communications specialists should work closely to formulate the emergency response plan. Along with the information that should be included in the emergency plan, it is proper to include a list of emergency communications specialists and those who are not assigned as such, but are capable of this service. The plan should include frequencies that you anticipate utilizing, including primary and back-up frequencies.

A BRIEF HISTORY OF EMERGENCY COMMUNICATIONS
IN THE CHURCH

      To understand the need for emergency communication among wards and stakes, it is beneficial to look at its origins. In June, 1976, the Teton Dam, located in southeastern Idaho, failed, flooding homes, causing deaths and destroying property located miles downstream. At the time, no emergency communication was established for such an event. As the flood progressed, it destroyed telephone lines – the only means of communication. There were no cell phones at the time. Consequently, there was no way to inform residents of the approaching flood, which caused still more deaths and destruction.

      After this event, the Church put a plan into motion, which included a network of ham radio operators. This plan has grown and matured, and over the years has expanded throughout the United States and some parts of Canada. Some areas are more active than others because of the obvious potential need for emergency communications (also called 'EmComm').

A term that is often used by emergency communicators within the Church is ERC which stands for Emergency Response Communications. This is in reference to an idea. It is not a program. The Church does not have an ERC department. It is simply a term that is used to identify ham radio activities (or, more accurately, emergency communications activities) that are conducted by Church members. For example, ERC net, ERC meeting, etc. This acronym is seldom used by non-LDS people. Consequently, it was adopted (or commandeered) to be used informally by Church members. Therefore, you may hear the term used, but it is not used in any official Church documentation.

TYPES OF EMERGENCY COMMUNICATIONS RADIOS

There are several methods of communication available for emergency use. For example, there is FRS, GMRS, CB, ham radio and others. Following is an explanation of each:

FRS – Family Radio Service – this is a simple radio system that is used commonly by families at theme parks and other events. The radios are sometimes called walkie talkies, or two-way radios. They can be purchased at Wal-Mart® and other similar retailers. No license is required. Their range is usually quite limited – less than a mile. The radios have 14 channels. Please refer to Appendix A on page 69 for specific FRS frequencies and other information.

GMRS – General Mobile Radio Service – These are similar to FRS radios, with 2 exceptions. First, an FCC family license is required. No test is required, but the FCC presently charges $85 for the license. Once obtained, any family member can use the radios to communicate with each other. There is no limit on how many family members that can use the family license. The range of a mile or so is similar to the FRS radio. The other difference is the fact that there are some GMRS repeaters that have been installed in some communities. These repeaters can be used by contacting the repeater owners and requesting permission. GMRS has 23 channels. The term 'repeater' will be explained later. Please refer to Appendix A on page 69 for specific GMRS frequencies and other information.

MURS – Multi-Use Radio Service – Similar to CB, but is limited to 2 watts. It has 5 channels. Please refer to Appendix A on page 69 for specific MURS frequencies and other information.

CB – Citizens Band – CB's have been around for decades, and are still in use today by truckers, jeepers and others. Their range is usually a few miles - not as limited as FRS and GMRS, but, through better antennas and other means, a range of 20 miles or more can be achieved. It has 40 channels.

21

Satellite Phone – This service is VERY expensive. Its dependability can also be debated in a real emergency. It requires a monthly subscription and is additionally charged on a per-minute basis during use.

Cell phones are sometimes useful in certain conditions, which vary, depending on the circumstances. In particular, texting may be functional when normal voice communications are not available.

Other resources, known as 'social media', such as Twitter, Skype and Facebook can be useful if internet service is available.

Although these choices have some utilitarian uses, ham radio is, by far, the most utilized method of communication in emergencies. Ham radio is also utilized by many other emergency services organizations and is recognized by them as the best way to communicate in such situations. This commonality between these organizations and Church members allows us to work well together in practice events, as well as in actual emergencies. Given these facts, we will focus on the use of ham radio.

HAM RADIO AS AN EMERGENCY
COMMUNICATIONS TOOL

Ham radio is well known as a hobby and as a form of emergency communication. There are over 700,000 ham radio operators in the United States. Other countries are also well represented with ham radio operators. You have probably seen ham radio shown in movies, using Morse Code. While Morse Code is still in use today, regular voice communication is the most popular use of ham radio.

Ham radio began as a hobby for experimenters who discovered that a signal could be transmitted through the air. As time passed, the U.S. Government discovered the advantages of this new invention. Eventually, rules were set up to organize and regulate frequencies for various users, including amateur radio operators.

HOW TO GET STARTED IN HAM RADIO

Ham radio is used throughout the world. Regardless of which country you live in, ham radio is regulated by government entities within each country. In the United States, the Federal Communications Commission (FCC) is the regulating body. An FCC license is required to operate a ham radio. There are presently three licenses that are issued. They are; Technician, General and Amateur Extra. The Technician license is the first license that is issued. In order to obtain a license, a multiple choice test is administered. The test for each level is progressively more difficult. Most people obtain the Technician license and do not pursue the General or Amateur Extra license. That is fine, because the Technician license is all that is required for most communications needs on a ward level.

The General and Amateur Extra class licenses provide privileges in ham radio bands that are useful for longer distance communications. This may be required for wards and stakes that are in mountainous areas or are larger in size. The ham radio bands in use by a General or Amateur Extra Class licensee are accessed by equipment that is much more expensive and, therefore, should be given serious thought before considering.

There are several methods to study for the FCC test. One method is called a ham cram. This method involves reading all possible questions that could potentially be on the test, and reading only the correct answer to each question. The 35 questions that will be on the test are taken from a pool of about 400 questions. Some ham radio clubs offer the test questions in this format. The ham cram method is usually administered by giving the student two to four hours to study the questions before administering the exam. Using this method, usually about 90% of those who participate will pass the test the first time. Admittedly, not much is learned about ham radio when using this method. Although additional follow-up training is needed to better understand the operation of a ham radio, it allows the communicator to get on the air and learn by doing. This is a perfectly acceptable way of obtaining a license. Learning more about ham radio will come over time from experienced hams.

A more popular, but time-intensive method, is to obtain a manual which explores the many subjects that are covered in the test and thoroughly teaches each concept in depth. Most manuals have about eight chapters. The teaching process is, therefore, broken up into eight lessons which are typically taught over an eight to ten week period. Once the instructor feels that the students are ready to take the exam, it is scheduled and administered by FCC volunteer examiners. Of course, the students need to feel confident that they are ready for the test. This can easily be determined. There are several web sites that allow the student to take a practice test online, free of charge. In fact, the test can be taken as many times as the student wishes. Some example test sites are:

http://www.eham.net/exams/

http://www.hamradiolicenseexam.com/index.html

http://www.aa9pw.com/radio/

http://www.qrz.com/ht/

An internet search for 'ham radio license testing' will lead you to additional sites.

A third method is simple – self-study. If the student is more comfortable studying the subject on their own, that's fine. When the student feels he or she is ready, an online practice test (as described above) is in order. A testing site can be located and the official test can be administered. You can locate a testing site by going to www.arrl.org and clicking on 'Exams'. You can search by zip code or many other criteria.

There are several sources for quality study manuals. Two organizations will be mentioned here. The first is from the American Radio Relay League, or ARRL. Their web site is http://www.arrl.org. There is currently a tab called Licensing, Education & Training. Click there and you will see books shown – one called the Ham Radio License Manual. As of this printing, the book's cost is $29.95 plus shipping and is worth every penny. In addition to test preparation, it can be used as a reference for years to come. Make sure you get the Technician Manual.

Another manual can be located by accessing http://www.w5yi.org and clicking on "Study Materials" on the left column. The first manual shown at the top of the list is the Technician Manual. Its present cost is $20.95 plus shipping. It is also an excellent reference manual.

Both the ARRL and W5YI sites are valuable resources for information regarding ham radio. When you are ready to take the FCC license exam, you will be charged about $15. As stated earlier, testing locations can be found at the ARRL and W5YI sites mentioned above. Your license is valid for your lifetime, but has to be renewed every 10 years. The renewal is free.

FREQUENCY BANDS

Let's talk about frequency bands. Each license level permits the licensee to have privileges of various frequency bands. A frequency band is defined as a set or group of consecutive frequencies which are designed for a specific purpose. That sounds complicated, but really isn't. Let's look at an example. The FM broadcast band that you commonly listen to at home or in your car has a frequency range from 87.5 to 107.9 MHz The 'MHz' will be explained later, but is an abbreviation for the term Megahertz. When an FM station is broadcasting on a frequency in the range described above, you are able to receive a local station which broadcasts within that frequency band.

Another example of a commonly used frequency band is the aviation band. This is a set of frequencies that are used by pilots and ground personnel to communicate with each other for the purpose of controlling air traffic. The range of frequencies for the aviation band is from 108.0 to 135.0 MHz. You will notice that the aviation band is immediately after (or above) the high end of the FM broadcast band.

There are several hundred bands which are organized for specific uses, a few of which are used by ham radio operators. The most common ham radio frequency band for beginners is 144.000 to 148.000 MHz. This does not sound like a very wide band – meaning – not a lot of frequencies. Actually, it includes a large number of frequencies when you consider that the three numbers to the right of the decimal can be utilized. This ham radio band is commonly called the 2 meter band.

Other bands include the 160, 80, 40, 20, 17, 15, 12, 10 and 6 meter bands. There are also the 1.25 and 0.7 meter bands. The 0.7 meter band is commonly called the 70 centimeter band. In addition, there are other bands which we will not mention at this time. The point is that there are literally thousands of frequencies available to the ham radio operator on about 15 bands. All of the frequencies of these various bands have specific characteristics. Some bands are used to communicate with other individuals who are thousands of miles away. Other bands will carry a signal only a few miles, but have other advantages.

In addition to licensing, all of the ham radio bands used in the U.S. are regulated by the FCC. Since we have the ability to communicate with ham radio operators in other countries, they must have similar rules. As stated, each country has its own licensing system. In order to coordinate the various bands and frequencies, an organization called the International Telecommunications Union (ITU) coordinates all frequency uses in order to provide proper management with all participating countries throughout the world.

WHO IS IN CHARGE & WHAT ARE THE PRIORITIES?

Let's explore the quotes from the Church's web site and explain some aspects of how emergency communications operate within the ward and stake.

First and foremost, we need to remember that our Priesthood leaders are just that – our leaders. As emcomm specialists, we should be guided by them and not them guided by us. Any emergency situation within a ward, stake or any other Church unit, should be led by the appropriate Priesthood leader. That should be without question. There may be times when you disagree with the way things are being done. Nevertheless, we need to support the Priesthood leaders in any and all situations. It is the duty of the Emergency Communications Specialist to provide communications support for those Priesthood leaders who preside over them.

When normal means of communications are available, such as phone, cell phone and texting, it is simply more practical to use those methods. Don't use ham radio when phones are available. This may seem obvious, but needs to be stated. There may be times when voice operations via cell phone are not available, but texting is available. If this is true, utilize this valuable form of communication.

The bishop and other Church leaders will want to know the status of members within their unit as soon as possible. This will speed up the process of providing the proper response – whether it be medical, or other resources that are needed. As stated earlier, the status of the full-time missionaries is a priority.

Next on the list of priorities are buildings. This includes Church property, as well as members' homes. Church buildings may be needed as shelters and will need to be assessed for such uses as soon as is practical. Members' homes will also need to be assessed in order to determine what is needed for members to get back to normal life.

In addition, the general status of the community at large needs to be assessed. Local priesthood leadership and Church Headquarters will want to know this. This information will be easier to obtain if we have developed a working relationship with local government leaders and emergency services personnel.

HAM RADIO EQUIPMENT

A practical method of acquiring ham radio equipment is to do so gradually. There are very few callings or assignments where a Church member needs specialized equipment that he/she has to purchase. As you purchase equipment, don't break the bank. It is not necessary to do this –

or this -

or this –

The first piece of ham radio equipment which will be most useful to you is a handheld radio. A single band handheld radio (also called 'HT' or 'Transceiver') will cost about $130. An example is shown below. There are several brands and several retail outlets that sell HT's. The term 'HT' stands for 'Handheld Transceiver'. The term 'Transceiver' is a combination of two words – 'transmitter' and 'receiver'. Listed below are just a few retailers that sell ham radio equipment:

http://www.hamradio.com

http://www.aesham.com

http://www.texastowers.com

Some radio brands include Alinco, Icom, Kenwood, Yaesu and others. There have recently been some Chinese made radios that have entered the market and are in the $50 to $100 range. It is highly suggested that you locate a ham radio club or individual in your area that can assist you in purchasing radios and other equipment. A ham radio mentor is commonly called an 'Elmer'.

An HT is very useful and can receive and transmit for several miles when transmitting to or receiving from another HT. Ham radios can also be used in conjunction with equipment called repeaters. The use of repeaters will be discussed later. The range of your HT can be greatly extended from a few miles up to 20 miles or more by using a repeater. To determine the effective range of an antenna, see the explanation and formula in Appendix B on page 71.

As you develop in your assignment as a communications specialist, you will probably want to purchase additional equipment which will allow more flexibility and increase your range of communications. This can be done gradually, which will be a smaller shock to your budget.

The next piece of equipment that is suggested is an antenna that can be temporarily attached to your vehicle. The best antenna to get is one that has a magnetic base, called a mag mount. There is a wire (called 'coax') attached to the mag mount antenna, while the other end is attached to your HT, using the proper adapter (more about this in the next paragraph). You simply remove the antenna that came with your HT and attach the mag mount coax to the radio. The roof mounted antenna will extend the range of the radio considerably. This HT/mag mount combination is very portable and allows you to install and use the radio in any vehicle or other location. The antenna that comes with the HT is affectionately called a 'rubber duck' because of its flexibility. Any auxiliary antenna that is used in place of the rubber duck will extend the range of the HT radio.

With regard to the adapter issue, there are three primary types of antenna connectors that are used with most ham radios. To explain these connectors, let's talk about an AC outlet. As you know, an outlet in any home is compatible with the plug that is connected to any appliance you wish to plug into an outlet. This compatibility allows us to be assured that we can use any AC powered item that comes into our home. This has not always been the case. Some of us remember the advent of grounded outlets.

Previous to grounded outlets, an adapter was necessary to plug a grounded appliance into an ungrounded outlet. But that's another story. Back to antenna connectors. Over the years, radio-to-antenna connectors have been standardized down to three types - SMA, BNC and UHF. The SMA connector is now the standard for most handheld radios. The BNC type is generally no longer used on newer radios, but is still in use on older radios. The UHF type is most often used on mag mount antennas and mobile radios. Mobile radios will be discussed shortly. It is sometimes necessary to acquire an adapter, the most common need of which is from a mag mount to an HT. When purchasing a mag mount, discuss with the retailer the possible need for an adapter. They will know which adapter is needed for your radio.

Following are examples of the three most common connectors.

        This is a BNC connector. Note the angled slot on the outside in the center. This allows the user to insert the connector into the radio and secure it with a quarter turn. Its approximate diameter is 3/10 of an inch.

This is a SMA connector. It is a fairly small connector with a fine thread. Its diameter is about 2/10 of an inch.

This is a UHF   connector. Its diameter is about
6/10 of an inch.

This is called a UHF barrel connector. It is used to connect two ends together that are male connectors. All connectors are gender specific.

36

The next suggested piece of equipment is an antenna that is permanently mounted to your home. Regarding antennas, the higher they are, the better the signal. We are not suggesting that you purchase a 100 foot tower and install an antenna on the tower. However, having an antenna at least above the highest point of your roof will improve your outgoing and incoming signals considerably, even while using an HT. In addition to the antenna, you will need the proper type and length of coaxial cable that will be attached to the antenna at one end and your radio at the other end. Coax can be purchased in 25, 50 and 100 foot lengths, with the connectors already installed on each end. It is a matter of determining the distance from the outside antenna to the location you plan to transmit inside your home. Again, consult with your elmer before purchasing or installing a home antenna and coax.

Coax comes in many sizes. The length has been previously discussed. The thickness is another issue. There are two conductors in coax wire. The inside-most conductor is called the center conductor, and the outside conductor is called the shield. These two conductors are kept separate and protected by plastic, foam or rubber insulation. All three components (the center conductor, the shield and the insulation) are available in different thicknesses. The thicker the conductors, the better signal strength you will have, or more accurately, there will be less line loss. On the other hand, the thicker the coax is, the more difficult the coax will be to handle, and the more expensive it will be. There is, then, a need to come to a trade-off between better signal (or less signal loss), and desired flexibility of the coax. Most coax has a minimum loss of signal strength up to 100 feet in coax length. You will probably not need a coax of more than 50 feet, so signal loss will be kept to a minimum.

Coaxial cable for ham radio operation is available in many sizes. Each size has its own model number. Some examples are RG-58, RG-8X, LMR-240, RG-213, 9913 and LMR-400. Below is a line loss chart, showing how much signal energy (DBI) is lost for 100 feet of coax. The bigger the DBI number, the greater the loss. The cable types are shown in order from small to large cable.

Cable Type	DBI Loss
RG-58	6.2
RG-8X	4.7
LMR-240	3.0
RG-213	2.8
9913	1.6
LMR-400	1.5

Another way to show the loss is by showing the relationship between power output in watts and the length of coax. The following chart also shows common types of coax available with their corresponding loss by length.

Length	Watts	LMR400	9913	RG-8	RG-213	RG-8X	RG-58
15'	10	9.496	9.478	9.223	9.138	8.684	8.406
25'	10	9.174	9.145	8.738	8.605	7.904	7.488
50'	10	8.417	8.363	7.636	7.404	6.247	5.606
75'	10	7.772	7.648	6.672	6.371	4.938	4.198
100'	10	7.085	6.995	5.831	5.482	3.903	3.143

It becomes obvious that as you read through the first list, the coax will be larger in diameter, since the signal loss becomes less. It's then a matter of choice as to which coax type will serve your needs, given the trade-off explained above. This is another good time to consult with your elmer and/or the ham radio retailer.

Next on the list of equipment is a radio that transmits with more power. Typically, an HT transmits with 2 or 3 watts of power. Another radio, commonly called a mobile radio, transmits with 50 to 75 watts of power. This added power will allow people to hear you quite well at a greater distance, and better than from an HT. Virtually all mobile radios use 12 volts DC power. As the name implies, a mobile radio can be installed permanently in a vehicle. If you decide to do this, your vehicle battery will provide the power to operate it. If installing a mobile permanently in your vehicle, you will also need an antenna. The mag mount can be used for this purpose. However, it is common to have a permanently mounted antenna installed.

A mobile radio can also be used at home as a base station. It works well, given the added power output compared to a handheld radio. However, it will be necessary to provide a 12 volt DC power source for the radio. There are two methods of providing power to a home installed mobile radio. The first method is to purchase what is called a power supply. This is plugged into the wall, using house current, and converts 120 volts AC power to 12 volts DC. A power supply works well with the mobile radio and will provide all the power you need for the mobile. It is highly recommended that you obtain a power supply that uses 'switching' technology. A power output of 25 amps is recommended. Most power supplies will show a voltage output of 13.8 volts DC. This is a standard voltage output, even though we often refer to the voltage level of 12 volts.

The other method of providing power for a mobile radio in the home is by using a 12 volt battery. If you are thinking of having to bring a car battery into the house and having battery acid leaking everywhere, that is not necessary. There is a variety of sealed batteries that will work quite well and will be very safe in the home. A fairly new battery technology, called Absorbent Glass Mat (AGM), works well for this application. An AGM battery is a sealed lead-acid battery that provides the assurance of safety.

If you have a battery, you will also need a battery charger. Once a battery is fully charged, it doesn't need to be continually charged. This may seem obvious, but there is a difference between a commonly used trickle charger and what is known as a battery charger/maintainer. A maintainer will monitor the battery and keep the charge 'topped off' without damaging the battery, which can happen if a trickle charger is left attached to the battery. Use the charger/maintainer system. Also, make sure the battery is compatible with the battery charger/maintainer.

If it sounds more complicated and expensive to have a battery and charger/maintainer, you are correct. However, there is an advantage to this configuration over a house current fed power supply for the radio. If the house power goes out, you will continue to have power for your radio. In fact, the battery will probably provide enough power for several hours, or several days, if the radio is used conservatively. Remember that you will be using less power while receiving than while transmitting, and even less while simply monitoring, and you will be monitoring most of the time. In addition, when your battery gets low, it will be relatively simple to remove a battery from your vehicle, put it in a safe place outside your home, attach it to your radio and you are back in business. It is possible to reinstall the battery into the vehicle, start the engine and allow the vehicle charging system to recharge the battery in an hour or so. This is very advantageous, because it allows you to keep operating, potentially for weeks, and still remain in your home with communications abilities, even without house power.

For local operation, this is probably the furthest extent you will need to go, as far as equipment. As a review, listed below is the equipment you may want to acquire on a gradual basis and in the following suggested order:

• Handheld Radio (HT)
• Magnetic Mount Antenna (Mag Mount)
• House Mounted Antenna
• Mobile Radio for House or Vehicle or Both
• Permanently Mounted Antenna for Vehicle
• Power Supply for in-house Mobile Radio, or
• Battery and Charger/Maintainer for an in-house Mobile Radio

A WORD ABOUT HF, VHF and UHF

All of the information regarding ham radio equipment thus far has been in reference to 2 meter radios. The 2 meter band is one of the bands within what is called 'VHF', which stands for Very High Frequency. Another commonly used band by technician licensed ham radio operators is called UHF, or Ultra High Frequency. One band in the UHF spectrum is the 70 centimeter band. The frequency range in the U.S. is from 420 to 450 MHz. This band requires a radio that will transmit and receive on the UHF frequencies. There are radios that are called dual band radios. They are designed to transmit and receive on two separate bands – the 2 meter band (VHF) and the 70 centimeter band (UHF), for example. These radios are more expensive and it is recommended that you seriously consider the advantages versus price of such a radio before purchasing one. Typically, the 2 meter radio will be quite adequate, especially for a beginner.

HF (or High Frequency) radios are typically used to communicate with people beyond the range of VHF or UHF, from a few miles away to halfway around the world. This capability is not usually needed on a ward level. On a stake level, it might be used to communicate with the Bishop's Storehouse who can then communicate with Salt Lake. In mountainous areas, HF may be the only way to reliably communicate. In addition, HF communications require a General or Amateur Extra license. The equipment is substantially more expensive. However, if such needs exist, it would be well to consult with experienced hams on how to proceed with venturing into the HF world.

SIMPLEX vs. REPEATERS

Up to this point, we have discussed ham radio equipment without discussing what methods you can employ to utilize them. The most basic and simple method is called voice. This simply means that when you transmit and talk into the radio, someone else who has a radio tuned into the same frequency will be able to hear your voice. In fact, anyone tuned in to the same frequency will be able to hear you – as long as you are within the range of the other person or persons. This is called simplex operation. A simplex frequency is one frequency being used by two or more people. For example, a typical frequency of 147.555 MHz can be tuned in on several radios. The operators of those radios will then be able to communicate with each other. Bear in mind that only one person will be able to talk at any given time. This is different from what we are used to while talking, for example, on the telephone. The phone system uses a method called duplexing, which allows us to talk over each other, in a manner of speaking. Despite the limitation of simplex, communicating in this way is fairly easy to get used to. Voice simplex operation is the most simple and easy to use method in ham radio.

Repeater operation is a bit more complicated. However, its advantage is that the range of a handheld or mobile radio will be greatly extended – 10 to 50 miles or more, versus just a few miles range in simplex operation. A repeater is a special radio which is positioned in a permanent location – usually on a hill, mountain or tall building. Two frequencies are used with a repeater. For purposes of this discussion, we will call them Frequency A and Frequency B. Using an HT, for example, you would transmit on Frequency A. The repeater receives the signal and then retransmits it on Frequency B. All those listening would be tuned into Frequency B and hear the signal from the repeater. Anyone responding would transmit on Frequency A and the same result would take place – all others listening would listen on Frequency B. The procedure of only one person talking at a time is the same as when using simplex operation. Switching between the two frequencies (A & B) is automatically done by the radio.

Repeaters are very common in most communities. They are owned by individuals and ham radio clubs. It would be wise to obtain permission from the repeater owner to use the repeater. It is not difficult to locate the owner. The person responsible for the repeater is called the repeater trustee. You can usually hear someone who knows the owner or trustee communicating on the repeater. Once the owner knows you, he will be happy to allow you to use the repeater.

Many repeaters are associated with, or have some sort of formal agreement with, specific emergency services organizations. This means that in an emergency situation, the repeater would not be available to anyone except those associated with the specific organization, or those permitted by the repeater trustee. This makes things more difficult for those who wish to use the repeater for emergency communications who don't belong to the emergency services organization. There are two solutions to this problem. The first is to have exclusive use of a repeater. The equipment costs are something to consider, along with repeater maintenance and the responsibility of monitoring it 24 hours a day because of potential misuse. The second solution would be to use simplex only. Depending on your needs with regard to range, this may be a solution. If your ward or stake is within a reasonable range, it is advantageous to meet on a simplex frequency and not rely on a repeater at all.

OTHER MODES USED IN HAM RADIO

Modes are defined as specific methods that are used by ham radio operators to convey a message. We have already discussed voice communications. Other modes and activities are listed below, along with a short explanation of each mode or activity. Voice communications are most common. Following are just some of the additional modes of ham radio operation you may want to be aware of:

CW – Continuous Wave, also called Morse Code

Digital – The ability to send and receive messages by linking a computer to a ham radio. Put simply, you are sending messages through the air, instead of through a telephone line – like an email.

D-Star – D-Star is presently offered only through ICOM brand radios. It digitizes a voice transmission before sending it out on the air.

APRS – Automatic Packet Reporting System – A method of connecting a radio to a GPS, allowing the user to automatically transmit their location by longitude and latitude. This information is received by someone who has a mapping program on a computer that can map the information and have a visual on the map of the location of the person or several persons.

ATV – Amateur Television – Attaching a video camera to a ham radio allows the user to transmit an image to someone who has a radio attached to a television or other video receiving device.

IRLP / Echo Link – Internet Radio Linking Project and Echo Link are cousins. They allow an operator to link to the internet through a repeater and connect to another repeater, which can be located anywhere in the world.

There are specific activities which hams commonly participate in. Some are:

EME – Earth Moon Earth – With the proper antenna and radio, this allows a person to aim and transmit a signal at the moon, which bounces off its surface and is received by someone who can see the moon at the same time the person transmitting can see the moon.

DXing – DX stands for distance. DXing means you are communicating with someone who is a long distance away, usually several hundred miles, or more.

Contesting – There are numerous contests throughout the year in ham radio; e.g. how many people you can contact in a 24 hour period, or other criteria.

Fox Hunting – It's like hide and seek. A small transmitter is placed in a hidden spot. The participants look for it by receiving the signal with their radio and determining what direction the signal is coming from, ultimately locating the transmitter.

Experimentation / Kit Building – Self-explanatory. Different types of experimentation take place, mostly antenna building. There are several companies that sell kits for radios and other devices. Building kits often allows the builder to learn more about electronics and how ham radios operate.

Public Service Opportunities – Many local events, such as marathon runs, cancer walks, air shows, public gatherings, etc. ask for ham radio operators to utilize their skills. They are placed at strategic locations at the event, allowing the people in charge to have instant communication in case there is a medical or other need for the participants.

Field Day / JOTA – Field Day is held on the fourth full weekend of June on an annual basis. It is the most popular contesting event of the year. Usually, ham radio clubs sponsor a local Field Day event where radios, antennas and related equipment are set up at a remote location. The needed electrical power to operate the radios is always emergency power – batteries, solar or generators. The event is used to determine readiness for a real emergency. The contest portion is designed to determine how many contacts that can be made in a 24 hour period.

JOTA is Jamboree On The Air and is a Field Day type of event which takes place on the 3rd full weekend of October. It is an effort to involve Boy Scouts in ham radio. Below are three web sites that provide more information about JOTA.

- www.scouting.org/jota.aspx
- www.arrl.org/jamboree-on-the-air-jota
- www.k2bsa.net/jota

NETS

A net is defined as a formal scheduled meeting on the air which is conducted for a specific purpose. It can be scheduled any time – say, once a week at a certain time. It can be held on a simplex frequency or on a repeater. Make sure you have permission from the repeater owner or trustee to conduct a net. The net is conducted for one or more specific purposes. Usually, the main purpose is to provide ham radio operators the opportunity to practice their communicating skills and to let the operator who is conducting the net provide instruction and assistance. That person is called the Net Control Operator. All communication is directed by Net Control.

Typically, he or she will have a printed introduction at the beginning of the net, called a preamble. It is suggested that the Net Control have a list of anticipated participants. For example: a stake has a number of ham radio operators that wish to meet for a net. The Net Control Operator can call each participant, one at a time, by ward and first name. The person would respond with their name and FCC call sign. After all on the list are called, the Net Control Operator can ask if there are any visitors who wish to check in. He may have one or more individuals check in who are not part of the ward or stake. That's OK. We want to make anyone who checks in feel welcome and invited. This promotes good will in the ham radio community.

After all have checked in, there can be a discussion on one of many subjects. Keep the subjects non-religious in nature. Use discretion in the conversation that is held. Remember that others are probably listening. There may be some training that can be provided, or just general chat. This will build confidence and communication skills in new hams. The net also provides the Net Control Operator several pieces of information. First, he knows who the active ham operators are, because of their consistent check-ins at each net. He also knows who he can depend on, should the need arise.

The net can be held on a repeater, then repeated immediately after on a simplex frequency. This will provide the

Net Control Operator with an idea as to who can be reached via simplex versus repeater operations. Another trick that will accomplish the same goal is to use the Reverse button on the radio. The Reverse button is on all radios. Consult your manual on where it is and how to use it. As stated in the Repeater section, two frequencies are used when utilizing a repeater. For example: you transmit to the repeater on frequency A and receive on frequency B. If someone else is transmitting and you press the Reverse key on your radio, this will allow you to listen to the other person on frequency A – the frequency that the other person is transmitting on. If you can hear him clearly, you are hearing him directly from his radio. This means that you could use a simplex frequency. There would be no reason, in this case, to use a repeater. This may sound confusing, but is easy to do once you try it.

If conducting a net, be consistent with the day and time. Make the net worthwhile and productive. This will encourage more participation. If there are any communication errors made by new hams, make gentle suggestions over the air. If needed, discuss problems over the phone, then try a test communication between you and the person you are helping. As you patiently guide new hams, they will appreciate it and will be willing participants.

Once you have identified some regular participants, give them the opportunity to conduct the net. This will provide them with the experience of conducting a net and will put the shoe on the other foot. Their perspective changes when they are conducting the net.

IS THIS A 'GUY' THING?

Many feel that ham radio is a hobby that only involves the male population. That is entirely untrue. Many women pursue ham radio because of their interest as a hobby or as an effective emergency preparation tool. It is also common to see a husband and wife obtain their ham radio license together. If you purchase a book for test preparation and you both learn at the same time, you will receive double the value out of the book. If you are both radio equipped, it is good practice to talk to each other. This allows much less formal conversation and provides confidence while practicing with someone you trust.

From the Church perspective, it is a great advantage to have female hams. They can more easily be utilized by the ward or stake Relief Society president, if needed.

Another interesting phenomenon is that the higher pitch of a female voice is usually clearer and easier to understand on the radio. Female hams make great net control operators.

In some cases, the entire family gets involved and earn their FCC licenses together. It is a great hobby and skill for all members of the family that will last a lifetime.

EMP (ELECTROMAGNETIC PULSE) - INTRODUCTION

Most disasters are well understood such as earthquakes, tornados, floods, civil unrest, etc. An Electromagnetic Pulse (EMP) event is not as well known, but is considered by many to be a definite possibility. As such, it would be wise to fully understand this threat and know how to protect your equipment in such an event.

There are two sources of an EMP event – the sun and a nuclear weapon. An explanation of each source and their effects are given in Appendix C and D on pages 73 and 79, respectfully. These explanations are quite lengthy, but provides a detailed explanation of EMP, its effects and how to protect your equipment.

HOW THE COMMUNICATIONS SPECIALIST OPERATES WITHIN A UNIT

Planning is of upmost importance

As stated earlier, the ward emergency preparedness specialist and the ward emergency communications specialist should work together closely for the purpose of formulating a written ward emergency plan. This should be done under the direction of the bishop, he being the Priesthood leader. If further guidance is necessary, it can be obtained from the stake emergency preparedness specialist, the stake emergency communications specialist, the high counsellor who is responsible for emergency preparedness, or the stake president.

Once the ward emergency plan has been written, it should be presented to the bishop and approved by him. He may wish to review it with the bishopric or ward council for the purpose of making key leaders within the ward aware of its existence, location and content. The plan should be reviewed and updated at least every 6 months.

The emergency plan should have a list of those in the ward who are prepared to function as emergency communicators and can communicate effectively in an emergency. To help train those individuals and keep them active in emergency communications, it is wise to conduct nets, exercises or other activities. This will also provide valuable experience for those participating. Such basic knowledge as the ability to program a radio is something that should not be learned during an emergency situation.

The stake emergency communications specialist is directed by the stake president, usually through the high counsellor who is responsible for emergency preparedness. The stake emergency communications specialist should provide advice and direction to the ward emergency communications specialists. He can also sponsor and conduct nets, provide training and other activities that will better prepare ward specialists.

Most emergencies will affect only one or two wards. If an emergency of this size takes place and emergency communications are needed, the stake president will want to be informed of what is happening. If the entire stake is involved in an emergency, the Area Seventy will want to be involved. The stake president has contact information for the Area Seventy. If many stakes are involved in an emergency, Headquarters in Salt Lake will want to know what is happening. Church resources can be provided, depending on the scope and severity of the event.

In a disaster situation where emergency communications are essential, the ward and stake emergency communications specialists need to be positioned at a location that is convenient to their Priesthood leader, namely the bishop or stake president. This is sometimes called shadowing. If the Priesthood leader is mobile and needs communication, the specialist should be prepared to provide that service immediately, being able to shadow, or follow him wherever he goes. Usually, the specialist will be near the Priesthood leader at the 'command center' that the leader has chosen. This can be a ward building, the Priesthood leader's home, or other location.

Being ready at a moment's notice is the hallmark of emergency preparedness.

THE GO KIT

A Go Kit is defined as a backpack, or other easy to carry bag or pack, which holds all the needed equipment to function as an emergency communications specialist. It is essentially a 72 hour kit for communications. It may contain as little as one item – an HT, or many items. Following is a list of possible items you could include in a Go Kit:

- An HT, including its manual

- A longer HT antenna for better transmitting and receiving

- A portable mag mount antenna

- A portable antenna (with proper hardware) for hanging in a tree

- Coax for portable antenna

- One or more small sealed batteries with the appropriate battery-to-HT hook-up cable

- Battery chargers for the HT and batteries

- A pad of paper and pens

- A map of your area

- A flashlight

- Water

You will notice that the above list somewhat corresponds with the list under the Ham Radio Equipment section. This is intentional. The equipment you already have, or soon will have, could be utilized in an emergency.

A few brief comments are in order about some of the items listed. As stated earlier, the 'rubber duck' antenna that comes with any HT is the least efficient antenna that can be used. It is a very good idea, then, to have extra antenna options available. There are after-market antennas that are longer (about 18 inches) and therefore provide better receive and transmit capabilities. In addition, there are wire and stick antennas available (usually about 5 feet in length) that can be deployed using several methods. One popular method is to tie a small heavy object, like a rock, to a small rope, and throw it over a nearby tree. After retrieving the rope on the other side of the tree, connect an antenna and coax to the rope and pull it up from the opposite side. A large tree can raise your antenna to an impressive height, allowing excellent receive and transmit capabilities. Many hams have invented ways to hoist antennas into trees for the very purpose of improving transmission and reception. Trees are not the only object that can be utilized for this purpose. However, when deploying an antenna using this method, NEVER use overhead electric wires for raising an antenna. Never deploy antennas near overhead power lines. Overhead power lines transmit electricity at thousands of volts and will cause instant death if you are in contact with any wire that touches the overhead lines. Always employ safe practices when deploying antennas outside.

It is common practice to be prepared with more than one power source. An HT has its own battery pack, which is part of the radio itself. There are small batteries (about the size of a couple of sandwiches) that are 12 volt DC and provide a much higher amp-hour capability. These batteries weigh up to 5 pounds. Therefore, consideration should be given as to whether carrying the extra weight is worth the advantage. If you are positioned in a stationery spot, the weight consideration is less of a concern. The overall point is that any extra power source is a good thing to have available.

When connecting outside power to an HT or mobile radio, remember to bring the proper connectors that will be needed. All HT's have a DC input. This input is used for both charging the HT battery and for allowing outside power to be utilized. Side note – When importing power from an outside source, most HT's are designed to transmit at a higher power, usually 5 watts, allowing you to have a slightly better range.

When preparing to import power from an exterior source, it will be necessary to locate and obtain an adapter that is compatible with the power input port on the HT. Radio Shack® is a good source for this adapter, as well as the manufacturer of the HT. The plug will probably come with a length of wire attached to it. There is usually no connector at the other end of the wire. This is where some type of plug will be needed that will be compatible with your outside power source. This is where you will have to make some decisions as to what type of plug you want to use.

A very common power connector in the ham radio world is called an Anderson Power Pole. One source is at www.powerwerx.com Most hams have equipped themselves with the Anderson Power Pole system. This has provided compatibility between hams, making it much easier to interconnect power between hams' radios and available power sources.

Anderson Power Poles are available online. The methods used to assemble them require special care for full compatibility with equipment owned by other ham radio operators. There is soldering and/or crimping involved, which requires special tools and skills. These skills can be learned. However, it is best to consult with your elmer regarding the use of Power Poles or any other type of power systems.

THE CHURCH'S COMMUNICATION ORGANIZATION

As previously stated, the emergency communication organization within the Church is always led by the Priesthood line of authority. The organizational chart below shows the line of communication when it is necessary to get a message from the ward to Headquarters via a non-conventional method (land line, cell, etc.). This is seldom necessary, since most scenarios will be contained within the boundaries of a ward or stake, and conventional modes of communication will quite often be available. However, it is good to know the entire upward (and downward) line of emergency communication if it becomes necessary.

It should be noted that this chart is not designed to show line of Priesthood authority. Rather, it is showing the line of communication for emergency communications purposes. Remember that emergency communicators do not have any authority over Priesthood leaders.

Lines of Communication Chart

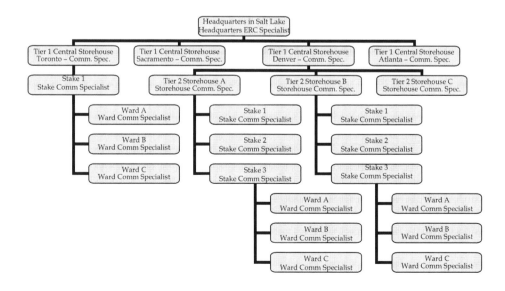

Assuming that all wards, stakes and storehouses had communications specialists, and working from the bottom up, you see that each ward's specialist reports information to the stake's specialist, and he, in turn, reports information to the storehouse specialist, and the information continues up the chain until the information reaches Headquarters, if necessary. This system should need to be operated only when other communications are not available. Otherwise, the stake president would contact the Area President or Headquarters by phone.

You will notice two layers in the storehouse level, and that they are either a tier 1 or tier 2 storehouse. As stated on the Church's web site, tier 1 storehouses are equipped with ham radio gear which is supplied by the Church. The tier 2 storehouses are not. It is easy to think of it as a hub-and-spoke system. The tier 1 storehouses are the hub. Several tier 2 storehouses operate through the tier 1 storehouse as spokes. For the purposes of emergency communications, and when needed, the tier 2 storehouses need to be manned by local communications specialists and with their own equipment. An example is also shown (see Tier 1, Toronto) which shows that all tier 1 storehouses also function as the storehouse for the stakes in the general area of that storehouse. There will be tier 2 storehouses surrounding the Toronto storehouse, as well.

Again, this table shows the line of communication, not the line of authority. We always respect the line of authority.

As a point of interest, there are approximately 26 tier 1 storehouses in the United States and Canada. The number of tier 2 storehouses that surround the tier 1 storehouses vary, depending on the area served. The same is true of the number of stakes and wards that are served by each respective storehouse.

WHAT SHOULD WE BE PREPARED FOR?

". . .if ye are prepared, ye shall not fear."

Doctrine & Covenants 38:30

The above chapter heading poses several thoughts. Most communities can expect repeated events, such as floods, earthquakes, tornados and other events. It is wise to prepare for the familiar scenarios. The unfamiliar ones are more difficult to prepare for.

It would be wise to study how disasters have been dealt with in the past. Hurricane Katrina was one of the most destructive and costliest ever. The following quote comes from Wikipedia:

"Volunteers from amateur radio's emergency service wing, the Amateur Radio Emergency Service, provided communications in areas where the communications infrastructure had been damaged or totally destroyed, relaying everything from 911 traffic to messages home. In Hancock County, Mississippi, ham radio operators provided the only communications into or out of the area, and even served as 911 dispatchers."

http://en.wikipedia.org/wiki/Hurricane_Katrina

Ham radio is not the only tool that can be used to help in such a disaster. The March 2011 Japan earthquake and subsequent tsunami flooded and destroyed north eastern Japan, affecting 20 prefectures (similar to U.S. states). There were 15,854 deaths, 26,992 injured and 3,155 people missing. After the flood water receded, paths were cleared for foot and scooter traffic, but were not wide enough for autos or trucks. The Church noticed that there was a need for scooters to get messages through and people moved. The following quote was taken from the Church's web site. The article is titled, The Scooter Miracle.

"In his first address at the April 2011 general conference, President Monson mentioned the great east Japan earthquake. 'Members are delivering aid via scooters provided by the Church to areas that are difficult to reach by car,' he said."

https://www.lds.org/church/news/chronological-report-of-church-operations-in-japan/the-scooter-miracle?lang=eng

Preparing for and dealing with disasters in unconventional ways may be necessary.

If we prepare properly for the events to come, we will be able to mentally face the challenges of the future. Some of those challenges may turn out to be other than normal or expected events. The old adage states that we should expect the worst and hope for the best. We should, when possible, prepare for any and all possible scenarios.

It is of upmost importance that we also be spiritually prepared. This is a task we can prepare for each day. When so prepared, we will find the peace that can be found nowhere else.

APPENDICES

A: Family Radio Frequencies and Power Levels

A = Column: Channel No. for 22 Channel GMRS Models
B = Column: Channel No. for 15 Channel GMRS Models
C = Column: Type of Radio Service
D = Column: Frequency in MHz
E = Column: Power in Watts a = 2.0 or less, b = 0.5

A	B	C	D	E
1	1	FRS/GMRS	462.5625	a
2	2	FRS/GMRS	462.5875	a
3	3	FRS/GMRS	462.6125	a
4	4	FRS/GMRS	462.6375	a
5	5	FRS/GMRS	462.6625	a
6	6	FRS/GMRS	462.6875	a
7	7	FRS/GMRS	462.7125	a
8		FRS	467.5625	b
9		FRS	467.5875	b
10		FRS	467.6125	b
11		FRS	467.6375	b
12		FRS	467.6625	b
13		FRS	467.6875	b
14		FRS	467.7125	b
15	11	GMRS	462.5500	a
16	8	GMRS	462.5750	a
17	12	GMRS	462.6000	a
18	9	GMRS	462.6250	a
19	13	GMRS	462.6500	a
20	10	GMRS	462.6750	a
21	14	GMRS	462.7000	a
22	15	GMRS	462.7250	a
		MURS	151.820	
		MURS	151.880	
		MURS	151.940	
		MURS	154.570	
		MURS	154.600	

B: How To Determine The Effective Range Of An Antenna

To determine range of VHF/UHF radios, a quick and dirty formula for knowing the distance you can talk is to multiply the height of the antenna by 1.5 and take the square root of that number. So a six foot person holding an HT will look like this - 6' x 1.5 = 9. The square root of 9 = 3 miles. This calculation will take you to the curvature of the earth on flat ground or the ocean. Two, six foot people on HT's will have a 6 mile range - that is, if nothing like hills or trees are in the way.

C: Solar EMP

There are many experts on the subject of EMP. One of those experts, Chris Beck, president of the Electric Infrastructure Security Council, has one of the best explanations. Following is an excerpt from a presentation Dr. Beck participated in:

"What kind of (solar) storm might we anticipate? We have geomagnetic disturbances all the time, and you've probably noticed there has even been in the media – and some pretty mainstream media – reports about this, because . . . the sun is entering an active part of its cycle. Every 11 years roughly, the magnetic field of the sun changes orientation. And when it does that, in the midst of that change, there are a lot of sunspots on the surface of the sun. When those sunspots form, those are basically areas of high magnetic field and they form loops. Those loops collapse and that action ejects charged particles from the sun – it changes fluctuation on the sun's magnetic field. It ejects charged particles and blasts them into space. Usually, those charged particles blast off into space and they don't really hit anything and there's not much of an impact. But every now and then, one of them is large enough and moving fast enough and happens to cross the earth's path – the earth gets in the way of one of these things. When that stream of charged particles passes by earth, it interacts with the earth's magnetic field, and then that causes the earth's magnetic field to fluctuate, and that, in turn, creates currents on Earth, and the best path for those currents to flow through is through our electric grid – especially the U.S. electric grid, because it is big, it is sophisticated, it was designed to have very low resistance, and so this is an ideal place for currents to flow.

"Now, you might think, well what's the big deal? I mean, yes, currents flow through the electrical grid and that's why it's there, right? It pushes electricity around and we all get to use it and our society depends on it. Well, the problem is that the electric grid is an alternating current system, and the fields that I'm talking about in the electrical field that are generated in the currents that these geomagnetic disturbances create are DC currents. So it's a different type of current, and when that DC current enters into an AC system, it causes the system to function outside of its normal parameters, and there are specifically, the grid components of concern are the very large extra high voltage transformers. They change the voltage up and down according to what is needed for a specific application. So, you want to have a very high voltage when you're pushing power through the grid long distances. Those are the very big transmission lines that you see when you're driving out on the highway – the real big ones. And then you have to bring that power – the voltage – back down when you get to somewhere that wants to actually use the power.

"Those transformers are the things that step up and down the voltage, and when DC currents get into the transformers – what's called bias – they sort of - if you want to think of it as, they sort of tilt, think of a platform. You raise one end and things start to slide down toward the other end. And that's kind of what happens – there's this bias voltage that sort of shifts everything in one direction when you have an alternating current that is used to moving back and forth evenly, it gets this bias, so it goes farther in one direction than the other, and that's not the way a transformer is designed to operate. So what happens is that some of the magnetic flux in the transformer leaks out and causes heating in the body of the transformer, and is the biggest concern is that you can have some damage.

"The other thing that it causes is what is called harmonics. Harmonics in the system cause – they're sort of like, think of a harmonic in the case of sound. You have a fundamental tone, and then an octave up is the harmonic of that tone. If you get the higher order harmonics, you have oscillations in there, in the system, that are not at the base frequency, and that causes problems with the electronics. It causes voltage instability, and you can get a power outage because of that.

"So the geomagnetic occurrence actually leads to two phenomenon that are both of concern. But it's around the question of the importance, the likelihood of this phenomenon that I think that NERC report discussed, and while we think both EIS Counsel, we believe that both of these phenomenon are important. It's clear

74

that one that damages these large transformers, in our mind, a much larger concern because, if those transformers are damaged, they will have to be replaced, and replacing large transformers - first of all they're expensive, they're several million dollars apiece, they're on the order of a couple hundred tons, they're not produced in large quantities in the United States, all the really big ones are all produced overseas, and they take about 12 to 18 months under normal circumstances when a company wants to get a new transformer – that's their waiting time when they order it. If a number of transformers are damaged, we would really have a serious problem in the United States, because all of the other infrastructures rely on electricity."

This dialogue was taken from an interview of Dr. Beck on Episode #96 of the EMPact Radio Show. It aired on April 11, 2012.

To sum up Dr. Beck's thoughts, electromagnetic storms emanate from the sun on a regular basis. Some are smaller than others. The major ones are called Great Geomagnetic Storms. The sun is a sphere. A storm can, and does, leave the sun in any direction. If these storms happen to be directed toward our planet, the earth will feel the effects of it. Minor storms are experienced quite often. Their effects can actually be seen in what is known as the Aurora Borealis, or Northern Lights.

A major storm was experienced in 1859. Richard Carrington, an amateur astronomer, observed a larger than normal amount of sunspots on the sun's surface. He saw what looked like an eruption, now called a Coronal Mass Ejection (CME), and 17 hours later, the effects were experienced on the earth. In 1859, the only electrical devices were telegraph lines and related equipment. However, the telegraph system was severely disrupted and, in some cases, destroyed. This event is known as the Carrington Event. It was reported that the Northern Lights could be seen from the equator and that a newspaper could be read at midnight in Denver from the light that was emitted from the solar storm. It is said that there were actually 2 CME's back to back, which took place in this event.

A final quote is from PBS's NOVA broadcast titled, "Secrets of the Sun". It originally aired in 2012. The following is an excerpt from the show:

"The solar storm carries a one-two punch. First is a solar flare, releasing an outburst of x-rays that can reach earth within minutes. The second, more ominous threat arrives a few days later – a phenomenon called a coronal mass ejection, or CME. It's a wave of billions of tons of electrically charged particles . . . Together, they could hit like a cosmic tsunami, delivering a surge of radiation and an electrical spike of trillions of watts, potentially crashing the power grid."

Regarding the 1859 event, the NOVA broadcast had to say this:

"Those two storms were not only enormous, but they happened one right after the other. No one alive has seen anything like it. If we had a geomagnetic storm of that intensity today, the National Academy suggests that the impact on critical infrastructure could be catastrophic. And the big, big concern is the electric power grid. The massive electrical surge from a CME wave could overload power lines and melt transformers, blacking out entire cities. Repair could take weeks, months and even in the worst case scenario, the National Academy suggests that up to 10 years for a full recovery. If that occurred – if you can imagine a world without electricity – you're really going back in time. It's not just the power grid that's at risk. More and more, we rely on technology that could be affected by the sun – global positioning satellites, long distance communications, airplane tracking, astronauts in space. So there's an urgency in understanding what it is that the sun is doing, what's it going to do next and how can we prepare for that and respond to it."

The National Academy referred to in the above quote is the National Academy of Sciences.

CME's have been experienced since the Carrington Event, including one in 1921 and another in 1989, both interrupting power. The 1989 event left 6 million people without power.

This phenomenon is said to have a cycle. Like a 100 year flood, or seasonal tornados, CME's have a time cycle that corresponds with the sun's solar cycle. In 2012 and 2013, the sun is expected to be at the high point of this 11 year solar cycle.

D: Nuclear EMP

The nuclear type of EMP event is less likely, but much more destructive. As stated, its origin is a nuclear bomb. The detonation of a nuclear weapon produces several effects or by-products, all of which are designed to destroy property and humans. First is the initial bright light. Anyone looking in the direction of a detonation will be instantly blinded. Another effect is heat. Anything within a few miles of the blast will be vaporized by heat, including metal and concrete. The next effect is wind. There is a tremendous wind which emanates from ground zero outwards, destroying everything in the path of the wind. Another effect is nuclear radiation, sometimes called fallout, which attaches itself to all objects in the immediate area, or is carried in the wind. It then becomes important to know which direction the wind is blowing in order to avoid the radiation. The last effect is electromagnetic pulse.

In 1962 the U.S. government experimented with a high-altitude detonation of a nuclear weapon in the South Pacific. Its code name was Starfish Prime. Other bombs were detonated as follow-up experiments. The first was launched to an altitude of 450 miles. Hawaii is located about 900 miles from the blast. Although there was little electronic equipment in Hawaii at the time, the effects were felt there. About 300 street lights were knocked out, and some telephone company equipment was damaged. It is quite likely that other countries who have nuclear weapons, have tested the effects of EMP as well.

EMP interacts with electrical devices – more specifically, integrated circuits - making them virtually useless. The strength of the EMP effect determines how useless the electronics become. Any device with an integrated circuit is vulnerable. It is easy to list those items: your watch, cell phone, computer, car, etc. On a wider scale, most electrical devices are controlled by integrated circuits, such as the pumps that provide water, process sewage, trains and trucks that transport food and all other items to their needed locations, gas supplies, etc. As noted in the solar EMP discussion, the national electrical grid is also threatened.

Nuclear weapons are normally detonated at a low altitude – usually within a few thousand feet of the earth. This proximity to the earth will cause the various effects to occur in a surprisingly small area – usually just a few miles from the epicenter of the explosion.

A much more effective and insidious method of using a nuclear weapon is to launch it into space. If exploded at an altitude of approximately 300 to 400 miles above the earth, and over the central portion of the United States, it is theoretically possible that such a placement would cause the EMP effect to occur throughout the U.S., southern Canada and northern Mexico. The other effects would not be felt or needed as an offensive weapon. Many think that under these circumstances, the EMP effect would render the entire country void of electronic and electrical devices.

It is easy to see that without electricity and all the modern conveniences that we now have, our lives would be drastically altered.

In normal life, let alone an emergency, it is vital that we have the ability to communicate. This ability allows us to be connected to the area around us and to distant locations. Even though most modern conveniences would no longer function in an EMP event, there are simple methods of protecting electronic devices. Since this is a discussion about communications, we will explore those methods.

The best method for protecting communications and other electronic equipment is to store them in a metal container which has a tight fitting lid. It can be a metal garbage can, a metal popcorn canister that is sold during Christmas season, or any other container that fits the description. It is the opinion of some that you should make sure that you line the container with an insulator, like cardboard, to prevent the electronic devices from making contact with the inner wall of the container. Others feel that an electric phenomenon, known as skin effect, makes it unnecessary to line the inside of the container.

On the outside of the popcorn canister where the lid mates with the canister, there is a layer of paint. Use sandpaper to remove the paint, allowing a metal to metal contact. Some have suggested ammo canisters as another possible container. There are also specialized bags that look like anti-static bags that hard drives are shipped in. These bags are sealable and are designed specifically for the purpose of protecting any electronic device from the effects of EMP. You can locate them on the internet by searching for EMP bags.

The term for the containers mentioned above is a Faraday Box or Faraday Cage. The internet has a large amount of data concerning this subject and how to build or assemble a Faraday cage of different shapes and sizes other than the metal canister type.

The reason for providing this information is to present you with as much knowledge as possible in order for you to prepare for such an event. What are the chances of experiencing such an event, and who would do such a thing? The answers are for another venue. There is additional information concerning EMP that is widely available. If interested, there is a podcast called EMPact Radio. This is a weekly radio show which interviews experts on this subject. It is possible to download the hour-long show and listen to those who have studied the EMP phenomenon for decades.

There are also government and non-government reports that have been commissioned and are downloadable free of charge. Following are current links to these reports:

http://empcommission.org

http://www.empreport.com/index.html

Additional internet resources regarding the EMP subject are:

http://en.wikipedia.org/wiki/Electromagnetic_pulse

http://www.fas.org/nuke/intro/nuke/emp.htm

One of the best pages the author has found, which gives tons of information on EMP's, tests, protection, etc. is the following:

http://www.futurescience.com/emp.html

Again, the reason for providing extensive information regarding the electromagnetic pulse threat is because it is little understood or known by most people. In order to identify and prepare for such an event, it is necessary to have the provided information. It is not difficult to integrate your preparation plans for other disaster scenarios with the EMP scenario. If you wish to learn more about this subject, there is a vast amount of valid information via the web. There is also a fictional book, based on all that is known about EMP. These facts are woven into a story, and provides a realistic view of what would happen in a community if such an event were to take place. The name of the book is One Second After, authored by William R. Forstchen.

E: Amateur Radio Operators are called 'Hams'

Have you ever wondered why we radio amateurs are called "HAMS"?

Well, it goes like this- the word Ham was applied in 1908 and was the call letters of one of the first amateur wireless stations operated by some members of the Harvard Radio Club.

They were Albert S. Hyman, Bob Almy and Peggie Murray.
At first, they called their station Hyman-Almy-Murray.
Tapping out such a long name in code soon called for revision and they changed it to HY-AL-MU, using the first two letters of each name.

Early in 1909, some confusion resulted between signals from amateur wireless HYALMU and a Mexican ship named HYALMO, so they decided to use only the first letter of each name and the call became HAM.

In the early pioneer unregulated days of radio, amateur operators picked their own frequency and call letters.
Then, as now, some amateurs had better signals than some commercial stations.

The resulting interference finally came to the attention of congressional committees in Washington and they gave much time to propose legislation designed to critically limit amateur activity.

In 1911, Albert Hyman chose the controversial Wireless Regulation Bill as the topic for his thesis at Harvard.

His instructor insisted that a copy be sent to Senator David I. Walsh, a member of one of the committees hearing the bill.

The Senator was so impressed, he sent for Hyman to appear before the committee He was put on the stand and described how the little amateur station was built and he almost cried when he told the crowded committee room that if the bill went through, they would have to close down the station because they could not afford the license fees and all the other requirements which were set up in the bill.

The debate started and the little station HAM became a symbol of all the little amateur stations in the country crying out to be saved from menace and greed of the big commercial stations who didn't want them around.

Finally, the bill got to the floor of the Congress and every speaker talked about the poor little station "HAM".

That's how it all started. You will find the whole story in the Congressional Record.

Nationwide publicity associated station HAM with amateurs.

From that day to this and probably to the end of time, in radio, an amateur is a HAM.

A much more plausible story, and the one presented by the ARRL, goes like this . . .

"Ham" – a "Plug" – A telegraph operator who is not proficient.

That's the definition of the word given in G.M. Dodge's "The Telegraph Instructor" published in the early 1900's as a guide for landline telegraph operators, in the days before radio. The definition has never changed in wire telegraphy.

Because the first wireless telegraph operators were landline telegraphers who left their offices to go to sea or to man the coastal stations, they brought with them their language and much of the tradition of their older profession.

In those early days of radio, spark transmitters were the norm and every station occupied the same wavelength – or, more accurately perhaps, every station occupied the whole spectrum with its broad spark signal. Government stations, ships, coastal stations and the increasingly numerous amateur operators all competed for time and signal supremacy in each other's receivers.

Many of the amateur stations were very powerful. Two amateurs, working each other across town, could effectively jam all the other radio operations in the area. When this happened, frustrated commercial operators could call the ship whose weaker signals had been blotted out by the amateurs and say "SRI OM THOSE #&$!@ HAMS ARE JAMMING YOU" (Translation – "Sorry, old man, those blankety-blank Hams are jamming you").

Amateurs, possibly unfamiliar with the real meaning of the term HAM, picked it up and applied it to themselves in true "Yankee Doodle" fashion and wore it with pride. As the years advanced, the original meaning has completely disappeared.

There is some confirmation of this second story, because G.M. Dodge's "The Telegraph Instructor" is a real book. It has been scanned into electronic format, and you can see the "Definitions" page here - **http://www.morsetelegraphclub.org /library/ files/html/dodge/dodge.htm#definitions**

Scroll down until you see "Ham". Notice that it refers to "Plug". Scroll down to "Plug" and you will see the definition – "A telegraph operator who is not proficient". Obviously this could have been construed to apply to the new radio telegraph operators, as well.

There are some other stories, as well, but with less credibility.

So, we will probably never know for sure where the term "Ham" came from. Personally, I think the second story has more of a ring of truth about it, but, you can pick whichever sounds better to you.

Whatever the truth, we are all still "Hams".

The second story was taken from the ARRL at http://www.arrl.org/ham-radio-history and the explanation was taken from The Citrus Heights VE Team Ham Radio Handbook, © November 2009.

- www.lds.org

- www.arrl.org

- www.nhnpreparedness.com/

- www.ocpreparedness.com/SitePages/Home.aspx

26667472R00055

Made in the USA
San Bernardino, CA
03 December 2015